Acknowledgements

KU-592-551

The publishers would like to thank:

Mrs. Sybil Ogilvie for first bringing the original edition to their attention.

They also gratefully acknowledge the assistance of:

John and Jane Adamson
Violet Bowler
Ronnie Buchanan
Ken Sterrett
Anne Johnston for the cartography
Jim Egner for cover illustrations
Jackie Hewitt ⎤
Ann Brown ⎰ of Farset Youth
and ⎱ and Community Development Ltd.
Avril Lyons ⎦

Belfast Central Library; The Linenhall Library; The Ulster Museum; Ulster Folk and Transport Museum; Ulster Society for Oral History.

Special thanks to:

Mr. R. Crane and Mr. W. McAuley for their courtesy and cooperation in the reproduction of this book.

The author would like to thank:

I would like to acknowledge the help and support of my wife, Joyce, who typed the manuscript and of my mother who proved an excellent oral history source on the subject of the blitz. Many other informants added a human dimension to the narrative.

The staff of the Public Record Office of Northern Ireland and of the Linenhall and Central Libraries helped in their normal efficient manner.

Any defects in the text are entirely the responsibility of the author.

Map of Belfast in 1941

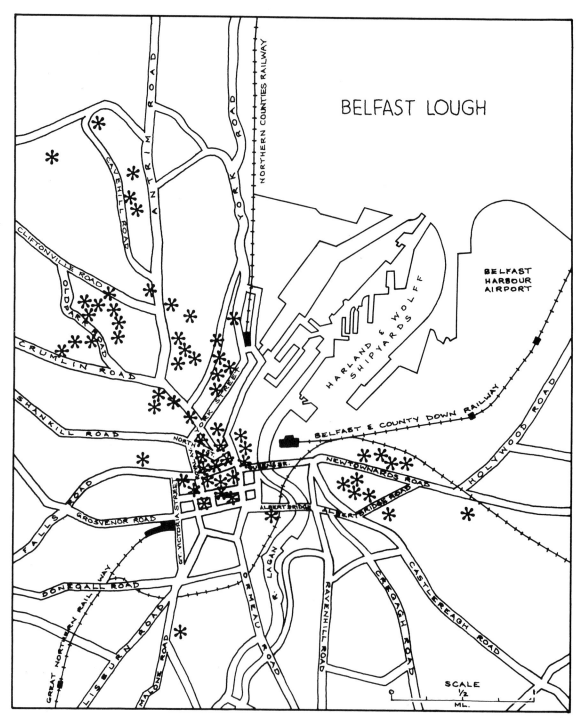

This map shows the locations of the photographs contained in the following section and indicates the main civilian areas affected by the blitz.

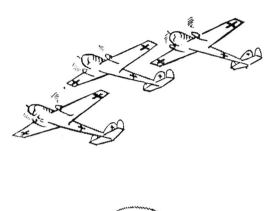

Introduction

It was inevitable that when the United Kingdom declared war upon the Axis powers on 3 September 1939 that Northern Ireland should play an invaluable role both in the defence of the realm and in the international fight against Fascism. As early as March 1938 the Northern Ireland Parliament had stated that,

'This house . . . assures the Prime Minister . . . that should any crisis arise, he can confidently rely upon the people of loyal Ulster to share the responsibilities and burdens with their kith and kin in other parts of the United Kingdom and the Empire to the utmost of her resources.'

War was welcomed by most of the citizens of Northern Ireland. Partly this was due to a feeling of patriotism amongst northern unionists, there was also a feeling that this was Britain's war and thus it was Northern Ireland's war. This would not be the case south of the border where Eire was maintaining a neutral stance. In 1937 it had underlined its independence by enacting a new constitution. Neutrality was not only popular within the southern state, but it also proved to be the most effective method open to De Valera of indicating the distinctiveness of the Irish nation.

In addition to the patriotism of northern unionists, there was the realisation in Belfast that the placing of the economy onto a war footing would greatly increase employment. In July 1935, for example, 101,967 people had been registered as unemployed in Northern Ireland; by February 1938 this figure had drop-ped to 92,000. Even so, this represented 29.5% of the insured industrial workers. Furthermore, an estimated 36% of the population lived below the poverty line.

Britain had commenced rearmament in 1935 and with it came the hope of employment without conscription. On 24 November 1936 Belfast was chosen by the Imperial Parliament as a major area of aircraft production. May of that year had seen the formation of a new company, an amalgamation of Harland and Wolff and Messrs Short Brothers, to be known as Short Brothers and Harland Ltd.

By the end of 1937 over 6,000 people were employed by the new firm. These were mostly in Belfast, but work was also carried out in outlying factories, most noticeably in Newtownards. Eventually some 20,000 people were to work for Shorts.

Initially, production was of the Bristol Bombay, a military transport, and the small Hereford bomber. However, endeavour quickly transferred to the Stirling long-range heavy bomber and the Sunderland Flying Boat. By the end of 1940 some 206 aircraft had been delivered and the factory at Sydenham was being described as the 'finest seaplane manufacturing base in the British Isles'.

Belfast's other major source of war effort was the Belfast shipyards, primarily Harland and Wolff. This firm had been founded in 1853 by Robert Hickson, who owned the Belfast Iron Works. He employed and subsequently sold the firm to a young man called Edward Harland. Harland in turn brought in a marine draughtsman called G.W. Wolff who subsequently became a partner. Harland's quickly grew to become one of the biggest shipyards in Britain and proved an invaluable asset to the British war effort during the Great War. It was only natural that the same firm would have a major role to play in the building of ships, both merchant and Admiralty, during the Second World War.

During the period from September 1939 to August 1945 Harland and Wolff and the other shipbuilding companies in Belfast, the most prominent being Workman Clark, built over 170 warships, notably H.M.S. Formidable and H.M.S. Belfast. They also repaired or converted over 3,000 vessels. In addition almost 500,000 tons of merchant shipping was launched. However, ships were not the only products of the yards. The New Ordnance Factory manufactured over 10,000 ordnance pieces from 1939 to 1943. In the same period some 505 tanks, 801 gun mountings and 13,250,000 aircraft parts were completed. Employment in these industries doubled, reaching a peak of over 30,000 people.

Northern Ireland produced other commodities which were of value to the war effort. James Mackie and Sons was re-equipped in 1938 with modern American machinery and commenced the manufacture of munitions. The Springfield Road factory was to become a major source of supply for Bofor shells. The Sirocco Works at the Bridge End produced heating and ventilation plant for the underground munitions factories in England.

Other products were turned out for the troops. The linen industry found its products required by the Ministry. Electrical wiring was also produced in the North. The bedding which the soldiers used and the clothing they wore were often made here. A number of small factories were engaged in such activities throughout the country towns of Northern Ireland. The long established shirt industry in Londonderry received large orders for battledress and this, coupled with the work in the dockyards, greatly decreased unemployment in the north-west. Later on the strategic importance of the port of Derry would prove invaluable to the war effort when in 1942 it was to become part of the U.S. Atlantic Fleet Command.

'the most unprotected city in the United Kingdom.'

We have seen the attitude of both the government and the population of Northern Ireland to the outbreak of war. The Unionist government was keen to demonstrate its fidelity to the British Crown in its hour of need. Most of the population felt the same way, and they also welcomed the additional employment which war production would bring. Belfast's industrial base was an important element in the war effort and one which would make it a possible target of the total war.

Nevertheless, there was a large degree of complacency within the city. The general population tended to feel that Belfast was too peripheral to the struggle to warrant German attention. So safe was Northern Ireland felt to be that once bombing commenced on the mainland over 1,000 people were evacuated from Eng-

land to "safety" in April 1941. Some of these were subsequently to die in the Belfast blitz.

This feeling of complacency was probably understandable. Initially Northern Ireland was outside the range of the German bombers, and even after the fall of France and the Low Countries in the summer of 1940, it was felt that the Germans would never risk flying the 1,000 mile round trip to attack Belfast. The population believed, as did the authorities, that they would never risk two crossings of the British mainland.

Nowhere is the attitude of the citizens of Belfast better evidenced than in the official evacuation figures. In the period up to 8 April only 12,095 people agreed to evacuation, and of these 5,053 had returned to the city by the time of the first raid.

This attitude was shared by the authorities who decided not to distribute Anderson air-raid shelters until such times as the two governments could work out the financial considerations. By the time the government recognised the threat to the well-being of the city it was almost too late. Belfast had the lowest shelter provision of any comparable city in the United Kingdom – a particularly dangerous situation for the city with the greatest density of population. In the first ten months of the war, for example, only 200 public shelters and 4,000 household shelters were erected.

The non-provision of shelters was not the only problem to be faced by the population, however. In March 1941, immediately prior to the first blitz, it was estimated that Belfast had only one-half of the anti-aircraft cover approved for the city. In all, Northern Ireland was defended by 24 heavy anti-aircraft guns, 12 light anti-aircraft guns, a small balloon barrage over Belfast and one over Londonderry, six radar stations, one fighter squadron based at Aldergrove and a Royal Engineers bomb disposal unit. Outside of Belfast, and to a lesser extent Derry, the province was undefended. And in Belfast itself the guns were only really capable of defending the area around the dockyards. In the whole of the country there were no searchlights, no night fighters, no special radar, no effective Observer Corp, no provision for decoy fires and no smoke screens.

In the summer of 1940 John MacDermott, the newly appointed Minister of Public Security, attempted to materially improve the defences of the city. In the Autumn of 1940 he commenced a frantic programme of shelter construction. In addition he discovered that a cabinet colleague had been returning the meagre ration of fire-fighting equipment to Britain on the grounds that it was not needed in Belfast. By now, however, all such supplies were desperately restricted. The Air Raid Precautions organisation had reported a year before, in June 1939, that it was unable to get the extra fire-fighting equipment due to general shortages. Furthermore, when eventually some large pumps and valves for fire hoses arrived there was no time to train the augmented Auxiliary Fire Service in their use. Thus when the Luftwaffe turned its attention towards Belfast it looked down upon a city which was well neigh defence-less.

Belfast's citizens could be excused for believing that their optimism had been vindicated. The German war machine had turned to the tactic of major aerial bombardment of British cities in October 1940. Whilst the cities on the mainland received nightly raids Northern Ireland was all but ignored by the Germans. This part of the United Kingdom was clearly not of such strategic importance that it would be in the front rank of the Luftwaffe targets.

Out of 146,717 civilians killed or seriously injured by bombs or rockets 80,397 were in the London Civil Defence Region. Also, for the first three months of the blitzkrieg, from September to November 1940, the vast majority of the raiders directed their attention towards London and the south-east of England. From November until the end of the year the bombs fell in a widening arc which took in the industrial Midlands. The frequency of raids decreased somewhat during December and January due to the inclement weather and when they resumed in February 1941 the main targets were the ports. Once again Northern Ireland appeared to have been ignored by all but the occasional marauder.

Ironically the first bombs to fall on Ireland were dropped by the Germans in August 1940 on a creamery in county Wexford. Three girls were killed and several others injured. The following month a single enemy aircraft made an unsuccessful attack on shipping off the county Down coast, and subsequently dropped a small number of incendiaries on the seaside town of Bangor. Later a ship in the town's harbour was damaged when struck by a drifting mine. On Christmas eve it was reported that the

previous week a small number of bombs had been dropped, causing minor damage. It seems likely that these and other similar incidents were the result of planes jettisoning their cargoes at random over Northern Ireland on their return flight from other targets. There had been no attacks to warrant the claim in a German newspaper that Belfast had been bombed in September 1940!

The reluctance of the Germans to attack Belfast is surprising. It is possible that even once Northern Ireland came within range, that the Luftwaffe was reticent about two crossings of the heavily fortified industrial Midlands of England. However, it also seems likely that Hitler was wary of the consequences of bombing the island of Ireland. Under the terms of Articles Two and Three of the 1937 Constitution, Eire claimed Northern Ireland to be part of its territory. It could be argued that to bomb Belfast was to infringe the neutrality of a strategically placed non-belligerent. The loss of the Eire ports had been a blow to the Allied Forces. The Germans might not have wished to risk offending Southern neutrality.

The first raid on Belfast, albeit a minor one, took place on the night of 7-8 April. It is likely that planes detached from the major raid on Clydeside to attack Belfast. This had the dual effect of testing the defences of the city prior to a major assault, and of being a diversion from the main target of the night.

Six Heinkel 111 bombers flew above Belfast at a height of 7,000 feet, safe from the barrage balloons. The He. 111c, a twin engined bomber with a crew of five, carried a bomb load of over 1,000 kg. The attackers initially dropped flares to light up the target which was clearly the Docks area. Showers of incendiaries were followed by high explosives and parachute bombs. These were directed towards Duncrue Street and the Queen's Yard. However, the fact that the planes were flying at such a height naturally took away from the accuracy of the bombing. Most of the incendiaries fell in east Belfast, on the Newtownards Road area from Templemore Avenue to the Albertbridge Road. Altogether 12 fires raged in the Ballyma-carrett area and St. Patrick's Church of Ireland was severely damaged.

The other area of residential housing close to the docks which suffered damage was the Shore Road and the Northern Road. Here again the small streets were showered with hundreds of incendiaries and a large parachute mine landed at Sunningdale Park, off the Cavehill Road. A first-aid post located at Grove School had to be moved to Mountcollyer School due to an unexploded bomb. Women extinguished many of the incendiaries with damp blankets and over in east Belfast one old lady, on seeing an incendiary come through her roof, calmly picked it up with a pair of fire-tongs and threw it out into the street.

A major fire was started in McCue Dick's timber yard on Duncrue Street whilst at Rank's Flour Mill the worst single incident saw the mill destroyed by a parachute mine with 15 people trapped, and nine killed. But the main target for the Luftwaffe had been the Docks area and on the whole the bombing had been accurate. The Victoria Shipyards at Harland and Wolff and the Alexandra Works were severely damaged. Just before the all-clear sounded, at 3:30 a.m., one of the raiders flew in low over Belfast Lough and dropped a parachute mine. It landed on the roof of the fuselage factory at Harland and Wolff's, totally destroying the 4½ acre site. This was the single most significant hit of the night, destroying jigs, machine tools and components for over 50 fuselages for Stirling bombers.

The defences of the city, without searchlights and with few anti-aircraft guns, offered little resistance. Over 800 shells were fired at the raiders from the various anti-aircraft emplacements. But because of the altitude of the planes no hits were claimed. One informant remembered the gunners at the Greencastle battery standing crying in sadness and frustration because there was nothing they could effectively do to prevent the destruction of Belfast. At another battery, Balmoral, an accident left one soldier dead and four injured.

However, the Luftwaffe did not get away completely unscathed. Four Hurricanes from 245 Squadron were scrambled from their base at Aldergrove to confront the raiders. Only one managed to do so. Squadron Leader J.W.C. Simpson was flying over Downpatrick, county Down, when he intercepted and shot down a Heinkel bomber.

Belfast quickly got over the shock of the first blitz. Generally the passive defences had coped well. The Fire Service had worked heroically in the Docks and Newtownards Road area, where two Auxilliary Firemen lost their lives fighting the flames. The Rescue and Casualty Services

had also performed adequately during this most minor of air-raids. War had come to Belfast and the city had acquitted itself reasonably well. Only 13 people had lost their lives that night. In addition 81 were injured, 23 of them seriously.

The morning following the raid large numbers volunteered for the Women's Voluntary Service, the Auxilliary Fire Service and the Civil Defence Corps. The requests for blood donations were intensified. An anti-aircraft battery and advance elements of some searchlight units were dispatched to Northern Ireland from Great Britain. Clothes and foodstuffs were stockpiled and another evacuation was planned for 16 April. The new moon, which had given the bombers light for the first blitz, would continue for some time and made for ideal bombing conditions. Experience on the mainland indicated that enemy aircraft usually hit the same targets more than once in a particular phased attack.

The first raid had been relatively light compared with others in England, Scotland and Wales, and life quickly returned to normal. The roads were cleared within two or three days and by the following week-end, Easter week-end, the population was once again settling down to normality. Thousands of trippers took the County Down Railway to Bangor to enjoy the fine weather. Back in Belfast, a representative soccer match was played at Windsor Park between the Irish Football Association and the Football Association of Ireland. Before a large crowd the local team won by two goals to one.

The following day, Easter Tuesday, Belfast citizens could choose between George Formby starring in 'It's in the Air', at the Royal Picture Theatre, or James Cagney in 'Torrid Zone', showing at the Ritz. Over at Windsor Park Linfield were defeated by near neighbours and arch-rivals Distillery by three goals to one. Few in the crowd would have seen a lone Junkers 107 reconnaissance plane fly over the city. If they had they would probably not have recognised it as a harbinger of things to come.

The plane was, presumably, sent to discover which areas of the city still remained unscathed by the previous week's bombing. It would also pay attention to the anti-aircraft emplacements. The Germans must have been surprised by the lack of opposition they had experienced in the first attack and a check was being made to see if any major augmentation had taken place. It had not. The fact that only one battery fired at the

107 (four shells, all of which missed their mark) must have confirmed the lack of real defence for Belfast.

'No other city in the United Kingdom, save London had lost so many of her citizens in one night's raid. No other city, except possibly Liverpool, ever did.'

Around 200 German bombers left their bases in Northern France and the Dutch Lowlands that evening. The attacking force was made up of Heinkel 111s which had undertaken the first air-raid, Junkers 88s and Dorniers. The Junkers were probably the Ju88A-4 model. This was the most common and effective Junkers plane in commission at that time. It was a high-speed bomber which could carry a 3,300lb bomb load and it had an increased defence armament. Information is not available about the Dornier model used in the attacks on Belfast but the Dorniers were, by and large, medium-sized bombers.

The sirens sounded at 10:40 p. m. on Easter Tuesday evening. The planes approached from the north-east between the Divis and the Black Mountain, sweeping low over the city. The first wave dropped flares to light up the target areas. It was followed by more waves carrying incendiaries, high explosive bombs and parachute mines. The latter were designed to destroy the pre-stressed concrete and steel which protected industrial targets.

As the flare-carrying Heinkels approached a dense smoke screen was released from the shipyards in an attempt to disguise their exact location. The Heinkels must have mistaken the Water Works for the shipyards, for the flares were dropped in the north of the city. Once the flares had lighted up a target, there was no return for the bomber pilots. From then until 5:00 a.m. the bombs would fall inexorably upon that area, principally in an arc from the Whitewell Road to the Crumlin Road. In particular York Street, Duncairn Gardens, Antrim Road and the Whitewell Road were devastated. Once again opposition was weak although H.M.S. Furious, at that time in the dry dock for repair, fired at the invaders throughout the night.

If it can be assumed that the primary target for the bombers was the industrial base of Belfast then the Easter Tuesday raid was only a limited success. The shipyards and docks area were relatively unscathed. Shorts suffered only minor damage with two aircraft being lost.

Damage to the harbour was slight, with only one parachute mine, four high explosive bombs and a number of incendiaries finding their target. A small fire was started in the Power Station which was quickly brought under control. The Frame Shed was damaged and the Alexandra Works, already damaged in the previous raid, was again hit, with the roof falling in. Within Harland and Wolff the bombers were more successful – the Boiler Shop, the Copper Shop, the Brass Foundry and the Bolt Screwing Shop were all hit. This coupled with the major damage experienced earlier, virtually stopped production in the shipyards.

Other commercial targets attacked included Ewart's Mill, Brookfield Mill, Edenderry Mill, and the York Street Mill. Brookfield and Edenderry were gutted whilst the York Street Mill was completely destroyed. The offices and stores of the L.M.S. station at York Street were destroyed and the rail lines were severed. A margarine factory in Hudson Street, McIlvenna and McGinley's mineral water plant in Bath Place and the Wilton Funeral Home on the Crumlin Road were all destroyed. As the true extent of the raid emerged the loss of one of the major funeral homes was most unfortunate.

A contemporary report of the damage indicated that 30 businesses, seven motor works, seven stores, two banks, two schools, two cinemas, two tram depots, two hospitals and the Mater Infirmorum Hospital Nurses' Home experienced various degrees of damage. The Ulster Hospital in Templemore Avenue which had suffered minor incendiary damage in the previous raid was hit by a large bomb which completely destroyed the new wing. One doctor who had retired for the night was awakened by the loss of the wall of the building in which he was sleeping. The bed remained perilously close to the edge but his shoes and stethoscope had to be recovered from the street outside.

It would be impossible to detail every major target for the bombers. Reports of hundreds of incidents can, however, be sifted through and the most significant described. In this way the depth of tragedy faced by the population can be examined.

Perhaps the worst single incident occurred after the bombing of York Street Mill, the largest spinning factory in Europe. Most of the wall on one side of the mill collapsed on top of the small mill houses in Sussex and Vere Streets. Altogether 42 houses in Sussex Street and 21 in Vere Street were destroyed with the loss of 35 lives. The death toll would have been considerably higher but for the efforts of two members of the Royal Ulster Constabulary. Together they pulled 60 people out of the remains of their homes, many of them still alive. One of the officers subsequently received the George Medal.

In the Shankill district a large number of people were killed in the shelter established at Percy Street Gospel Hall. A local councillor, Alderman William Boyd, was in his house in Percy Street at the time. His brother Hugh had returned from Bangor to see if the family was well. Just after he arrived at the house a bomb shattered the windows and blew him off his feet. His father then persuaded Hugh and his brother Elias to go to the Percy Street shelter. They were unable to gain admission to it as it was completely full. A moment later a bomb fell about 15 feet from the shelter, demolishing it. About 60 people died in this one explosion including the two young Boyds. They were found outside the shelter without even a scratch on them. Alderman Boyd, who subsequently became the Northern Ireland Labour Party member for Woodvale, remembered that shortly before the bomb fell his father had a premonition that he would lose two members of his family that night.

The story of destruction, desperation, panic, courage and carnage continued in almost every small street in north Belfast. In Ballynure Street, off the Oldpark Road, 16 people (nine from one family) were killed when a bomb landed on the house in which they were sheltering. In Veryan Gardens two parachute mines fell almost simultaneously. Over 120 houses were damaged with 46 residents losing their lives. The injured totalled 118. After the dust settled hundreds ran in panic down the Whitewell Road to the local shelter. Casualties were taken to Stag Hall House, to the shelter at 88 Whitewell Road, to Graymount First Aid Post and, when these were full, the injured were tended in the open fields.

Frank Danby was a warden in the Whitewell Post. He asked permission to return to his house to see if the members of his family had survived. The occupants included his mother and father who had returned to Belfast from the south-east of England to avoid the blitz there. Just after he entered the house a bomb landed on it killing all the occupants.

A similar tragedy occurred at 45 Veryan Gardens. The McKay family went to the house of their friend Daniel Doherty and together they decided to shelter in the fields nearby. On reaching the field it was discovered that Dan Doherty was still in his house. His family then decided to return to find him. When they did not return the McKay family followed suite. Just as they were leaving the house it was hit by a bomb and completely destroyed. Soldiers inspecting the damage later saw some movement and uncovered the youngest member of the Doherty family lying underneath his dead father. He must have been in his father's arms when the bomb landed and was protected by his father's body.

The next morning a small boy was discovered roaming alone in the fields nearby. He was unable to tell the authorities who he was or where he lived. The *Belfast Telegraph* published a photograph of him and he was subsequently identified by his aunt. His name was Brendan McKay and in the excitement to discover what had happened to the Dohertys he had been left in the field. This chance of fate saved his life. Hugh Doherty and Brendan McKay were the only survivors of the two families.

One of the major centres of damage was the Duncairn Gardens/Antrim Road area. It has been estimated that almost one third of the houses in the lower Antrim Road were damaged. In Hogarth Street which runs parallel to Duncairn Gardens whole blocks of houses disappeared in the cloud of dust and rubble, 45 being killed in 77 houses. In number 29, eight members of the Gordon family died, whilst in nearby Edlingham Street at the home of the Wilsons a similar number perished. The value of the communal shelters was shown in Edlingham Street where everyone inside a shelter escaped injury when a 250 kg high explosive bomb fell a few feet away.

Duncairn Gardens received a number of direct hits both from high explosives and from showers of incendiaries. St. Barnabas' Church of Ireland was razed to the ground and a parachute mine hit the corner beside the Co-operative store, killing the Renton family and a number of servicemen who boarded in the house. The servicemen had been outside helping others who had been injured. Mrs Renton called them in to have a cup of tea and it was while they were in the house that it suffered a direct hit. There were no survivors. Next door seven members of the Warwick family also died.

In one of the small streets between the New Lodge Road and Duncairn Gardens a mother crouched with her two young sons, one on either side, on a mattress under the stairs. An explosion in the street outside sent a blast up the hall which killed both children, each clinging to their mother's side, but left the mother unharmed.

By 4:00 a.m. the entire north of the city appeared to be ablaze. One aid post dealt with 150 casualties during the night whilst the officers at another had 40 injured under their care at one time. The shelters held up reasonably well. There had been the major loss of life in Percy Street and in addition all the wardens in Clifton Street shelter were killed when it experienced a direct hit. In the west of the city, a bomb hit a post in Eastland Street, killing two wardens and six civilians. Another 14 died when the shelter at Thorndyke Street collapsed under the shock of a nearby bomb. Shelters were not built to withstand direct hits but to protect people from injury due to bomb blast and falling masonry.

The shelter at the corner of East Bridge Street and Oxford Street withstood a parachute mine nearby. This bomb, however, was a particularly devastating blow to the city. It hit the telephone lines and from then, 1:45 a.m., until the 'all-clear' sounded at 5:00 a.m., Belfast was virtually undefended. All contact was lost with the mainland and communication was broken with the Gun Operating Control Room thereby silencing the anti-aircraft batteries. Fighter Sector Cross Channel Command was also unable to discover the nature of the attack on Belfast and thus no Hurricanes were sent across to engage the bombers. There was nothing Belfast could now do but sit and wait for the Germans to run out of bombs. Altogether 203 metric tonnes, along with 800 fire-bomb canisters, were dropped on the city that night.

While bombs were falling on Belfast minor raids were made on Bangor, Newtownards and Derry. Two parachute mines fell upon a group of Ex-Servicemen's Homes in the Maiden City, killing 15, with a similar number injured. In Newtownards bombs fell upon the aerodrome, killing three and injuring five. In Bangor high-explosive bombs and incendiaries killed five persons in Ashley Gardens and injured another 30.

Rescue work was seriously impeded by the damage done to the city. The loss of communication meant that messages had to be carried from area to area by motorbike or cycle. In addition many of the roads were blocked. The Albertbridge, Oldpark, Cliftonville, Cavehill and Antrim Roads and Carlisle Circus were each blocked either by bomb craters or rubble and many of the other arterial routes in the city were virtually closed. Donegall Park Avenue, Cliftonpark Avenue and Wellington Place were impassable due to unexploded bombs. Tram lines were down, numerous gas fires burned unattended in the streets and the authorities had to turn off the gas supply to almost the entire city. The bombing of the Water Works had reduced water pressure throughout the entire area and this problem was exacerbated by 32 major water line fractures which forced the authorities to turn off all water supplies to a large area of north Belfast. These circumstances jointly contrived to impede rescue operations, the major fear being that if the numerous fires were not soon brought under control the entire city would be burnt to the ground.

The 200 local appliances which were valiantly fighting the fires in Belfast needed some assistance, no matter how small. Fred Barry, the Duty Officer that night, recalled 20 years later that to this end the City Commisioner of Police, R. D. Harrison, recommended to J. C. MacDermott that help be requested from Dublin. By 4:30 a.m. a telegram had been sent to the Town Clerk of Dublin asking that southern brigades help fight the Belfast fires. By 6:00 a.m. word was received that aid was being sent immediately.

The swift reaction of the Southern Irish Prime Minister, Eamon De Valera has surprised some commentators. De Valera was awakened in the middle of the night with the message that Belfast was burning and immediately ordered as many southern brigades as possible to travel north. His action was more than humane. Eire was a neutral power during the conflict and such a decision could have compromised that stance. However, the Taoiseach could also argue that, as the Constitution of the state claimed that the Irish nation was synonymous with the entire island, the German bombing was an infringement of neutrality. Some days later he explained,

"... we are one and the same people – and their sorrows in the present instance are also our sorrows; and I want to say that any help we can give them in the present time we will give to them whole heartedly, believing that, were the circumstances reversed, they would also give us their help wholeheartedly."

In all 13 brigades from Dublin, Dun Laoghaire, Dundalk and Drogheda travelled to the North. They concentrated their help in the Crumlin Road area with engines also fighting fires in York Street and the Holywood Arches in the east of the city. They worked tirelessly but they were badly prepared, having no waterproof clothing. They were withdrawn just as dusk fell on 16 April, presumably for fear that another raid would cause loss of life and make a difficult position for the Irish Government even more problematic. The firemen carried back to the South stories of the destruction and most were overwhelmed by the large numbers of dead, both humans and animals, lying in the streets throughout the capital.

As well as the much needed aid from Dublin, 32 appliances were despatched from Glasgow and ten from Liverpool. Altogether 400 firemen arrived from these two cities and they remained in Belfast for five days.

The next few days were spent in clearing up the debris, rescuing the trapped, tending to the injured and identifying and burying the dead. Altogether almost 900 had died with another 1,500 injured, 400 of them seriously. The extent of the casualties caught the authorities unawares. The hospitals efficiently treated the injured under the most trying conditions. But the number of fatalities was a different problem. The city mortuary was unable to cope with the large number of bodies. In an attempt to ease the situation corpses were also taken to St. George's Market near Cromac Square and to the Falls Road Baths. In the baths the bodies initially arrived in coffins and were laid out around the pool. However, the city quickly ran out of coffins and the baths became so full that bodies had to be accommodated in the swimming pool itself. The story in St. George's was much the same. Bodies would be brought in and tagged if they were unidentified. Over the next few days a constant stream of people arrived at the centres to identify and claim the bodies, hoping no doubt that their loved ones would be found elsewhere. Identification was difficult. Many of the bodies were hardly recognisable as human beings at all. One volunteer in the Falls Baths remembers a particularly large and odd shaped shroud being brought in. It was labelled, 'Believed to be a mother and her five children.'

After three days the bodies started to smell due to decomposition. This difficulty was particularly acute at the Baths. The problem was that there was still a large number of bodies unclaimed. It was decided to remove all the bodies to Mays Fields and lay them out on the grass where they could still be identified. So as to slow down the decomposition process an A.R.P. volunteer sat all day watering the bodies with a garden hose.

The week-end after the bombing, 21 April, there was a public funeral for 150 of the dead, 123 still unnamed. The cortege, on the back of five army lorries, travelled through the streets of the city and up the Falls Road, and the people of the city, both Protestant and Catholic, turned out in their thousands to pay their last respects. So many coffins passed that people inevitably lost count, giving the impression that the procession was unending. At the City Cemetery the cortege divided and the bodies of the Protestants were taken into the graveyard. The remainder, the Catholics, continued up the road for burial at Milltown. The problem of deciding which of the unidentified were Protestant and which were Catholic was said to have been solved by searching their clothes for religious medals and rosary beads. As in life so they were in death.

Immediately after the second blitz Belfast's defences were augmented from the mainland. Fire-fighting equipment and pumps arrived as did the advanced elements of two searchlight regiments. In addition one heavy anti-aircraft battery was transferred from Londonderry.

On the morning after the attack MacDermott initiated another major plan to evacuate the city. The Hiram Plan was brought into operation immediately. The purpose of the Hiram Plan was to return Belfast to 'normalcy' as quickly as possible after a heavy raid. Royal Engineers were brought in to help free the trapped and to demolish or shore up buildings deemed to be unsafe. Roads had to be cleared, burst water mains repaired and the gas supply to large areas of the north of the city reinstated. On that day it was estimated that some 40,000 people were homeless and that 70,000 had to be fed in the special centres set up for that purpose.

An immediate exodus started from the city. Over 100,000 people left Belfast, with the help of lorries commandeered for the purpose, for other parts of the Province. Special trains took others to Dublin, where over 500 received care from the Irish Red Cross under special arrangements reached between the two Governments. The town of Dromara, for example, saw its population increase from 500 to 2,500. In Newtownards, Bangor, Larne, Carrickfergus, Lisburn and Antrim many thousands of Belfast citizens took refuge either with friends or strangers.

In addition to the evacuees some 10,000 people walked to the countryside outside Belfast every night and slept in the open air rather than face another blitz. These people, known as 'ditchers', continued this nightly trek for some months.

Apart from the efforts to relieve the suffering of the population of the city after the second blitz, other measures were enacted to further protect the citizens of Belfast. For example, the law stated that only those persons living in houses with a Poor Law Valuation under ú13 could receive free shelters. After the blitz of 15-16 April this figure was raised to ú29. This immediately facilitated the erection of a further 26,000 shelters in the city at the expense of the government. It was widely expected that the Germans would return to the city to complete their task. They must have realised that whereas the degree of suffering inflicted upon the inhabitants had been immense, they had failed in their efforts to cripple the industrial base of the city.

The Hiram Plan was continuing to adminster the evacuation of people from the city and it was recognised that the Ministry of Public Security could not complete the task alone. Thus the Ministries of Education and Home Affairs lent a hand, especially in the welfare and evacuation of the homeless. For fear of a break-out from Bellevue Zoo, it was decided to shoot the dangerous animals. It was also recognised that the city desperately required more anti-aircraft guns and better fire-fighting equipment. Some success was achieved in the former area. It has been estimated that by the time of the third raid anti-aircraft protection had doubled. However, the Fire Service was still faced with shortages. Steel pipe fittings which had been requested by MacDermott the previous autumn had still not arrived. The situation had improved but the Germans did not give the city much of a respite

before launching their further assault upon Belfast.

At 11:45 p.m. on the night of 4 May the air-raid sirens once again warned of the approach of enemy aircraft. Once again Belfast was the major target of the night. This time there were few who remained in the upper stories of their homes to view the attack. By the time the first bombs fell, at 1:02 a.m., all but the essential services were sheltering. The planes came in from the north-east and the south. On this occasion they did not drop flares. The night was very clear and bright and the nature of the attack would in itself light up the target area. The bombers were also more cautious and they attacked from altitudes of 9,000-13,000 feet. This attack was known as the 'Fire-Blitz' due to the large number of incendiaries used. The bombers dropped over 200 metric tonnes of explosive but in addition the city was sprinkled with almost 96,000 incendiary bombs.

Unlike the previous bombing the German planes hit their targets. Major damage was inflicted on the harbour estate, the shipyards and the aircraft factories. The Alexandra Works, which had been hit the previous month, was once again severely damaged. In the Queen's Works high-explosive bombs brought down almost the entire roof. The sheet metal works in the Clarence Works was completely destroyed by the mixture of high explosives and incendiaries. In Abercorn Shipyard three corvettes which were near completion suffered direct hits. A transport ship in Dufferin Dock, the Fair Head, was sunk and blocked the fairway for a number of months. The Power Station within the estate was destroyed and the city was to be without electricity for the next 24 hours.

Short Brothers and Harland was also affected but not to the same extent as the shipyards. It was subjected to thousands of incendiaries. The stores, offices, workshops and flight shed were all damaged. Production of Stirling bombers was greatly slowed and it was over a year before full night work resumed, primarily due to the impossibility of effectively blacking out the factory.

No work was carried out in the yards for two days so widespread was the destruction. There were 77 areas of damage especially in the electric department. In addition there remained nine unexploded bombs to be dealt with. No other shipyard in Britain was so devastated in one night. In the first week following the attack production rate was only 10% but by the end of the third week this had increased to 40%. Four-and-a-half months later production was running at 60%, other Admiralty work at 50%, the Engine Works at 80% and the Electric Works at 90%. It was to be six months before the shipyards would return to full production.

The raid had been planned as an attack upon the industrial capacity of Belfast. In its aim it was a resounding success. Every important factory or industrial site charted by the Luftwaffe in November 1940 had by now been either destroyed or seriously damaged. The yards and aircraft works had enjoyed most of the attention. However, once again the civilian areas of the city suffered, many of them still recovering from the April raids. The Newtownards Road, York Street, Clifton Street, Bridge Street, Duncairn Gardens, Crumlin Road, Millfield and the Whitewell Road were the most affected. Their proximity to the major target area left them vulnerable. On the other hand much of the damage to non-strategic targets might not have been accidental. During the raid on Harland and Wolff six aircraft detached themselves from the main formation to rake York Street with cannon fire.

Within an hour the fires were completely out of hand, notwithstanding the efforts of the Fire Service. Equipment was sparse and as with the April blitz water supply was affected. There were 67 major water breaks. The authorities recorded two conflagrations, 22 major fires, 58 serious fires and 125 small fires. The largest fires were at Harland and Wolff, Short Brothers, the oil depot and Skipper Street. Overall the most fire damage took place in the York Street area. At 2:30 a.m. the City Commissioner asked that Dublin be contacted and be requested to send aid to Belfast. This was done immediately and once again 13 brigades made the journey from the South to aid the citizens of Belfast. At 3:00 a.m. the Home Secretary in London was asked to supply 50 water pumps.

One of the most vivid descriptions of the fires over Belfast came from a German broadcaster, Dr. Hermann Weninger, who flew in one of the aircraft. He described the situation as follows,

'When I arrived over Belfast I could hardly believe my eyes. As we approached the target at 2:30 a.m. we stared silently into a sea of flame such as none of us had seen before. In Belfast there was not a large number of conflagrations but just one enormous conflagration which spread over the entire harbour and industrial area.

Here were the largest shipbuilding yards. Here was the last hide-out place for unloading war materials from the United States. Here the English had concentrated an important part of their war industries because they thought themselves safe far up in the North of Ireland, safe from the blows of the Luftwaffe.'

The biggest single tragedy occurred in the Whitewell Road area. Almost simultaneously two parachute mines fell on Barbour Street. One landed on the house of Nurse Stacey at 74 Whitewell Road. Moments before she had been advised by the wardens to seek shelter from the bombs. She refused on the grounds that her daughter was due to have a baby and could not be moved; nor would she leave her. Minutes later the house suffered a direct hit which demolished it and the Orange Hall next door. Immediately after the dropping of the two large mines the area was subjected to a hail of stick bombs. Thirty people were killed and a large number injured. After the blitz one child was still unaccounted for. In a 25 foot deep bomb-hole a child's scooter was discovered half buried. Underneath, completely covered by debris was a little girl, unharmed.

Once again the churches of the city did not remain unscathed. Clifton Street Presbyterian Church and Duncairn Methodist Church were destroyed. The population of Belfast assumed that the Germans believed that munitions and medical supplies were stored in the churches. On the Falls Road some people saw this factor as an indicator that God was a Catholic!

In addition to the two churches three hospitals were hit. The Benn Hospital at Clifton Street was damaged but the Ulster Hospital at Templemore Avenue was all but completely destroyed. Further out to the east, military hospital No. 24 situated at Campbell College, was also bombed. In this incident a number of patients were killed. It was rumoured that one of the pilots was a former pupil whose father had worked in Belfast before the war.

Casualties were low compared with the previous raid. One hundred and fifty had been killed this time with 157 seriously injured. This was due primarily to the more efficient bombing of the targets by most of the German bombers. However, the evacuation of 100,000 people and the more realistic attitude of those who remained were also factors in minimising the casualties. In addition the air defences had been improved. This meant that the Germans had to fly at almost twice the altitude of the previous raid to avoid anti-aircraft guns which fired twice as many shells as in the previous occasion.

They broke off the attack at 3:40 a.m., no doubt pleased with the success of their second major mission over Belfast. At 4:35 a.m. the 'all-clear' was sounded and people ventured onto the streets to inspect the damage. The task of the volunteer services still lay ahead. As with the previous blitz there were difficulties of access to affected areas. However, the phone system was intact and communication was easier. The arrival of the southern fire brigades had helped push back the flames of the numerous fires. The smaller number of civilian casualties, about one-sixth of the previous raid, took much of the pressure off the casualty services. The 'Fire-Blitz' was a strike against the harbour area, and notwithstanding the attacks on some civilian areas the authorities were more able to cope with the aftermath.

The following night, 5-6 May the air-raid warnings once again sounded. Three or four bombers, presumably strays from the major force which was attacking Clydeside, dropped bombs on the city. The red alert was sounded at 12:35 a.m. and it was not cancelled until 3:38 a.m. A parachute mine was dropped in Belfast, falling near two communal shelters in Ravens-croft Avenue. These collapsed with the loss of 14 lives; a considerable number were injured. A number of firebombs were also dropped on the city causing isolated fires and casualties.

This raid, coming on the evening after the major 'Fire-Blitz', had a profound psychological effect upon both the citizens of Belfast and the rescue services. Many of the fires from the previous night still blazed. Dead bodies remained in the debris awaiting retrieval. Some of the injured were still trapped in the ruins of their homes.

The raiders did not get away without loss. Squadron Leader Simpson, who had shot down a Heinkel in the previous raid, was flying in from the sea off Ardglass, Co. Down, when he found himself heading directly for the first of three Junkers 88s. Almost instinctively he opened fire on the leader which, on being hit, rapidly lost altitude and exploded in mid-air over the sea. Shots were exchanged between the other two German planes and the Hurricane but no further damage was caused to either.

Altogether 191 people were killed in the two May raids. The seriously injured totalled 186 with a further 615 slightly injured. As with the April raid there was a public funeral. However, it was much smaller than the first.

There were to be no further raids on the city

On 30 May the Luftwaffe once again returned to Ireland. This time they bombed Dublin. The bombs fell mostly in the North Strand/Amiens Street area. Thirty-four people were killed and over 90 were injured. The Irish Government suggested that the culprits had been the R.A.F. but this was subsequently disproven and compensation was eventually paid to Ireland by the government of West Germany. Belfast offered to send brigades to Dublin to help fight the fires but the Irish authorities deemed such aid unnecessary.

Belfast had been ill-prepared for the blitz. Most of the equipment needed was centred on south-east England and the Midlands. There was no night-fighter squadron in the Province, only a small day-fighter squadron. There were no search-lights, nor was there any means of decoy. At the start of the war Belfast had 16 3.7 inch heavy anti-aircraft guns and six 40 mm light anti-aircraft guns. A comparison shows that to Belfast's 16 heavy guns Liverpool had 96, Glasgow 88, and Bristol 68. Further, there were only five flights of balloon barrage. The defences of our city, in other words, were totally insufficient. This was due partly to the inability of the Corporation, at that time almost bankrupt, to take the defence of the city seriously enough, and partly to the fact that much of the available material was already channelled towards the South-East and the Midlands. In the Autumn, immediately before the blitz MacDermott had requested vital supplies for the fire service but they still had not arrived by the end of May.

Another failing was in the provision of shelters. The shelters would not save people from a direct hit, but they gave considerable protection from shrapnel and falling masonry. The lax **attitude towards the provision of adequate shel**ter within the city contributed to the large number of fatalities caused in the raid of 15-16 April. It should be concluded, however, that with the meagre resources at its disposal the Government coped reasonably well. The one arm to government which failed abysmally was the Mortuary Service. Not enough thought had been given to the logistics of collecting, preparing, exhibiting and finally burying the victims of the bombs. In fairness it must be stated that no one expected a blitz to cause so many deaths

Nor was the population as active as it should have been. There was a widespread feeling that Belfast would never be bombed. German planes would have to fly almost to the extent of their fuel resources and more importantly cross the mainland twice. This apathy was indicated by the fact that when the Government organised an evacuation of 17,000 women and children from the city in July 1940 only 7,000 turned up. In the second evacuation, the following month, only 1,800 of the proposed 5,000 evacuees came forward.

The great advantage of involvement in the war had been the stepping up in industrial and agricultural production and the resulting increase in employment opportunities. Acres of tillage, for example, almost doubled between 1939 and 1943. Output of dairy products, livestock, vegetables and apples increased dramatically. Greater mechanisation and the use of fertilisers also took place. The war effort, in short, revolutionised and modernised the agricultural industry in Northern Ireland.

Industrial development was also marked. The output of munitions, aircraft and shipping was substantial. Employment in shipbuilding, aircraft and engineering increased from 27,100 in 1938 to 70,200 in 1945. The industrial base of the North of Ireland was greatly expanded.

But the very fact that Northern Ireland entered the war whilst Eire did not may have been the most significant aspect of the conflict. South of the border neutrality became one of the cornerstones for the distinctive ethos of the state. De Valera steered Eire through the vicissitudes of a war which at times threatened to engulf her. Withstanding considerable pressure from America and to a lesser extent Britain, Eire asserted her distinctiveness from the rest of the Commonwealth.

Just as the non-participation of Eire in the war had a profound effect upon southern Irish society, the commitment of the North was equally important. The chagrin of the Unionist government at the refusal of Westminster to introduce conscription in Northern Ireland was lost in a sea of patriotic resolve. The ports became bases for war shipping. Belfast and Londonderry contained escort protection groups whilst the latter also became part of the U.S. Atlantic Fleet Command. Airports were constructed rapidly and by 1943 almost 150,000 American troops were billeted in the North. The trauma of war and the different responses north and south further underlined partition. As Professor John A. Murphy has noted, 'it widened a gulf which had long since yawned between nationalist Ireland and Northern Unionists'.

Five British Empire Medals and one George Medal were awarded and over 20 commendations for bravery were made. Some 25 members of the civil defence were killed during the blitz; in addition a large number were injured – 44 of them seriously. The newspapers abounded with stories of strangers risking their lives for others, of acts of heroism. In the shelters Catholics repeated the rosary whilst Protestants sang hymns. At the public funerals Protestant and Catholic cried together. After the exodus from the city in the aftermath of the April blitz 'ditchers' did not question each others religion. As, Tommy Henderson, the Independent Unionist M.P. for Shankill pointed out in the Northern Ireland House of Commons.

'The Catholics and Protestants are going up there mixed and they are talking to one another. They are sleeping in the same sheugh below the same tree or in the same barn. They all say the same thing, that the Government is no good.'

The response of the Government to the threat was not simply one of incompetence. Admittedly they had been slow to realise the real threat of German bombs, but so, too, had the entire population. They had to contend with the impossibility of laying their hands upon the necessary equipment and the fact that in the face of concerted aerial attack upon densely populated civilian areas, civilian authorities could do little.

The material effect upon Belfast was immense. In bombing the city the Germans had struck a small but significant blow against the British war machine. By the end of the raids millions of pounds had been lost by interruption of production. The target of the two significant raids was the docks. Clearly the Germans wished to put them out of action. As noted above, Dufferin Dock was blocked for several months when the Fair Head was sunk in the middle of the fairway. In addition, Alexandra works, other shops in the harbour estate and the Short Brothers and Harland complex were destroyed. Production was drastically reduced in many areas for some time although this was generally rectified within a number of weeks. On the other hand the port was able to continue to function. This was particularly important when it is remembered that Belfast played a crucial role in the Battle of the Atlantic.

In terms of the population of the city, some 56,600 houses had been hit, 3,200 of them completely destroyed. Over 100,000 were made homeless and thousands were fed in the emergency rest centres. The May raids also led to large scale evacuation. According to government records on 15 May 900 people continued to shelter in halls in Lisburn, 2,000 in Dunmurry and 330 in Irish Red Cross centres in Dublin. By July there were 50-60,000 official evacuees but by Christmas this had dropped to 26,000.

One side effect of the blitz was that the social conditions under which the urban poor lived were brought home to people in rural and middle class areas for the first time. The government estimated that upwards of 5,000 people were 'absolutely unbilletable'. This was in addition to the billetable who were reported to suffer from fleas, head-lice, enuresis and inferior personal hygiene. The Moderator of the Presbyterian General Assembly commented,

> 'I have been working for 19 years in Belfast and I never saw the like of them before. If something is not done now to remedy this rank inequality there will be a revolution after the war.'

He further declared some of the victims fortunate that the houses they had been forced to live in were now destroyed.

The great cost, of course, was in the loss of life. Almost 1,000 people had perished, 2,500 were injured, many of them seriously. The scars inflicted on the population of the city have not completely healed. Oral history interviews indicate how vivid the memories of April and May 1941 remain. Men and women joined forces to fight abroad realising that there was a possibility that they would never come back. The loss of a loved one at their own fireside somehow was much harder to accept.

During the four raids on Belfast over 1,000 metric tonnes of explosive fell on the city. In addition the aircraft dropped 96,000 incendiaries on the night of 4-5 May alone. The photographs which follow, mostly taken by John Bonar Holmes of the *Belfast Telegraph*, provide a vivid picture of the destruction caused to the city. Many of the familiar landmarks disappeared. But the real suffering was experienced by the ordinary citizens of our city. *Bombs on Belfast* is their story.

Dr Christopher McGimpsey was born in Newtownards and educated at Campbell College, Belfast. He did his undergraduate degree at Syracuse University, New York where he graduated with a B.A. with Honors in American Studies. His PhD from the University of Edinburgh was for a thesis on Ulster reactions to the Home Rule movement. A former Fellow of the Institute of Irish Studies at Queen's University Belfast, he has published works on sectarianism and orangeism in North America and Ireland. A contributor to newspapers and journals in Ireland, he is currently working on a number of research topics.

He is married with four sons.

Belfast Telegraph

THIRD SPECIAL

70th YEAR [REGISTERED AT THE G.P.O. AS A NEWSPAPER.] SUNDAY, SEPTEMBER 3, 1939. THREE-HALFPENCE

BRITAIN AND FRANCE AT WAR WITH GERMANY

FORMAL DECLARATION OF HOSTILITIES

"The following official communique was issued from 10 Downing Street: On September 1 His Majesty's Ambassador in Berlin was instructed to inform the German Government that unless they were prepared to give His Majesty's Government satisfactory assurances that the German Government would suspend any aggressive action against Poland and were prepared promptly to withdraw their forces from Polish territory, His Majesty's Government would without hesitation fulfil their obligations to Poland.

At nine this morning His Majesty's Ambassador in Berlin informed the German Government that unless not later than 11 a.m. to-day (British Summer Time) satisfactory assurances to the above effect had been given and had reached His Majesty's Government in London a state of war would exist between the countries from that hour.

Shortly after eleven the Prime Minister said: "This country is at war with Germany."

France delivered a final ultimatum to Germany demanding that German troops withdraw from Poland. The ultimatum expires at five p.m. (B.S.T.).

The British and French Ambassadors formally bade goodbye to von Ribbentrop.

PREMIER'S STATEMENT

"LONG STRUGGLE TO WIN PEACE HAS FAILED"

HITLER WOULDN'T HAVE IT

ONLY FORCE CAN STOP HIM

"WE HAVE CLEAR CONSCIENCE"

THE Prime Minister broadcast on Sunday at 11-15 a.m. He said:

"I am speaking to you from 10 Downing Street.

"This morning the British Ambassador in Berlin handed the German Government a final Note stating that unless the British Government heard from them by eleven o'clock that they were prepared at once to withdraw their troops from Poland a state of war would exist between us.

"I have to tell you now that no such undertaking has been received and that consequently this country is at war with Germany.

"You can imagine what a bitter blow it is to me that all my long struggle to win peace has failed.

"Yet I cannot believe there is anything more or anything different that I could have done that would have been more successful.

"Up to the very last it would have been quite possible to arrange a peaceful and honourable settlement between Germany and Poland. But Hitler would not have it.

"He had evidently made up his mind to attack Poland whatever happened, and although he now says he put forward reasonable proposals, which were rejected by Poland, that is not a true statement.

"He can only be stopped by force and we and France are to-day in fulfilment of our obligations going to the aid of Poland, who is so bravely resisting this unprovoked attack upon her people.

"The proposals were never shown to the Poles, nor to us, and though they were announced in the German broadcast on Thursday night Hitler did not wait to hear comments on them, but ordered his troops to cross the Polish frontier the next morning.

"His action shows convincingly that there is no chance of expecting that this man would ever give up his practice of using force to gain his will.

"We have a clear conscience. We have done all any country could do to establish peace.

"The situation in which no word given by Germany's Ruler could be trusted and no people or country could feel itself safe had become intolerable, and now we have resolved to finish it. I know you will all play your parts with calmness and courage.

"At such a moment as this the assurance which we have received from the Empire are of profound encouragement to us.

"After I have finished speaking, certain details will be announced of the plans the Government have made and I ask you to give them your close attention."

The Premier concluded:

"Now may God bless you all. May He defend the right. It is evil things that we shall be fighting against—brute force, bad faith, injustice, oppression and persecution, and against them I am certain that the right will prevail."

THEATRES TO CLOSE

SPORTS GATHERINGS TO CEASE

DRASTIC OFFICIAL ORDER

RECRUITING IN BELFAST

R.A.F. VOLUNTEER RESERVE

THE Government have given instructions for all cinemas, theatres, and other places of entertainment to be closed immediately until further notice.

SPORTS GATHERINGS, INDOOR OR OUTDOOR, WHICH INVOLVE LARGE NUMBERS CONGREGATING, ARE PROHIBITED UNTIL FURTHER NOTICE.

CHURCHES AND OTHER PLACES OF PUBLIC WORSHIP WILL NOT BE CLOSED.

RECRUITING REOPENED.

Recruiting is open for the R.A.F. Volunteer Reserve, and volunteers may present themselves at the Town Centre, Donegall Chambers, Belfast, to-day.

Acting on orders, recruiting had been stopped yesterday, but this order has been countermanded and recruits will be accepted as usual.

A number of men made application on Saturday and had to be turned away, but if these men return any time to-day or to-morrow their applications will be taken.

Many young men, including a number of Queen's University students, have enrolled this morning.

DOCTORS TO REPORT.

Doctors under the Ministry of Health Emergency Medical Service who were asked to report automatically for whole-time duty at specified hospitals should now report accordingly.

HISTORIC SUNDAY PARLIAMENT

Stresses The Nation's Oneness

HOUSE OF COMMONS, Sunday.

Of the momentous statements which Mr. Chamberlain has made to the House of Commons during the last few days that which he made to a packed House to-day surpassed all.

The Speaker took the chair at twelve o'clock.

When Mr. Chamberlain entered the Chamber at five minutes past twelve the whole House rose and cheered him. He smilingly acknowledged their greeting.

After some formal business the Prime Minister rose to make his eagerly-anticipated announcement at 12-6.

The PRIME MINISTER said:—

"Mr. Speaker,—When I spoke last night in the House I could not but be aware that in some parts of the House there were doubts and some bewilderment as to whether there had been any weakening, hesitation, or vacillation on the part of his Majesty's Government.

"In the circumstances I make no reproaches, for if I had been in the same position as hon. members on those Benches, and not been in the position of having the information which we have, I might have felt the same.

"The statement I have to make this morning will show that there is no ground for those doubts. (Cheers.)

"We were in consultation all day on Saturday with the French Government, and we felt that the intensified action which the Germans were taking against Poland allowed of no delay in making our position clear.

"Accordingly we decided to send to our Ambassador in Berlin instructions which he was to hand at nine o'clock this morning to the German Foreign Secretary, which read as follows:—

THE ULTIMATUM.

"Sir, — In the communication which I had the honour to make to you on September 1, I informed you on the instructions of his Majesty's Principal Secretary of State for Foreign Affairs that unless the German Government were prepared to give his Majesty's Government in the United Kingdom satisfactory assurances that the German Government had suspended all aggressive action against Poland and were promptly to withdraw their forces from Polish territory, his Majesty's Government in the United Kingdom would, without hesitation, fulfil their obligations to Poland.

"Although it is now more than twenty-four hours ago, no reply has been received, and German attacks on Poland have been continued and intensified.

"I have, therefore, to inform you that unless not later than 11 a.m. British Summer Time to-day, September 3, satisfactory assurances to the above effect have been given by the German Government and have reached his Majesty's Government in London, a state of war would exist between the two countries as from that hour."

"Sir, that was a final Note. No such undertaking was received by the time stipulated and consequently this country is now at war with Germany.

"I am in a position to inform this House that according to arrangements made between the British and French Governments the French Ambassador in Berlin is at this moment making a similar demarche also accompanied by a definite time-limit.

"The House has already been made aware of our plans, and as I said the other day we are ready. It is a sad day for all of us. For none is it sadder than for me. (Subdued cheers.)

"Everything that I worked for, everything that I had hoped for, everything that I believed in during my public life has crashed into ruins this morning. There is only one thing left for me and that is to devote what strength and powers I have to forwarding the victory of the cause for which we have to sacrifice. (Cheers.)

"I cannot tell what part I may be allowed to play myself, but I trust I may live to see the day when Hitlerism has been destroyed and a restored and liberated Europe has been re-established. (Cheers.)

THE LABOUR DEPUTY CHIEF.

Mr. GREENWOOD, Deputy Leader of the Opposition, said:

"The atmosphere of this House has changed overnight. Resentment, apprehension, and anger reigned over our proceedings on Saturday night aroused by the fear that delays might end in national dishonour and sacrifice of the Polish people to German tyranny.

"Those feelings, I have reason to believe, were shared by large numbers of people outside, and from messages which have come to me this morning what I said last night met with the approval of our people.

"This morning we meet in an entirely different atmosphere, one of relief, one of composure, and one of resolution. (Cheers.)

"The intolerable agony and suspense from which all of us have suffered is over. We now know the worst. The hated word 'war' has been spoken by Britain in fulfilment of her pledged word

Air-Raid Warning Given

THE Air Ministry announces: At 11-30 a.m. an aircraft was observed approaching the South Coast of England.

As its identity could not be readily determined an air raid warning was given.

It was shortly afterwards identified as a friendly aircraft and the "all clear" signal was given.

When the Speaker took the chair in the House of Commons at noon a siren in the vicinity could be plainly heard sounding the "all-clear signal."

and unbreakable intention to defend the liberties of Europe.

"We have heard more than the word spoken. We have heard war begin within the precincts of this House. I feel that I must in the name of my honourable friends—I think I may say in the name of the whole House and the whole of our people—pay tribute to the great restraint shown by Poland in the recent weeks.

"The last 54 hours have been proof that her restraint was not due to cowardice, but to her firm conviction of the rightness of her cause.

POLAND HAS STOOD ALONE.

"For 54 hours Poland has stood alone at the portals of civilisation defending us and all three nations and all that we stand for and all that we hold dear. She has stood with unexampled bravery, with epic heroism, before her hesitant friends have gone to her aid.

"Poland we greet as a comrade whom we shall not desert. To her we say, 'Our hearts are with her and with our hearts all our power until the Angel of Peace returns to our midst.'

"Lastly, in this Titanic struggle, unparalleled in the history of the world, Nazism must be finally overthrown.

"The Prime Minister has given us his word that so long as that relentless purpose is pursued with vigour, with foresight, and with determination by the Government, so long there will be a united nation.

"But should there be confused counsels, inefficiency, and wavering, then other men must be called to take their place. We share no responsibility in the tasks—tremendous tasks—which confront the Government, but we have responsibilities of our own which we shall not shirk.

"We have given proof in this Chamber during the past few days that we will give whole-hearted support to the measures necessary to equip this State with the powers that are desired. That support pledging this House will continue.

"In other directions, according to our opportunities, we shall make our full contribution to the national cause. (Loud cheers.)

"May the war be swift and short and the peace which follows stand proudly for ever on the shattered ruins of an evil name."

SIR ARCHIBALD SINCLAIR.

Sir Archibald Sinclair, Leader of the Liberal Opposition, said:

"I feel sure that at this grave moment when we have listened to the moving speech of the Prime Minister we should all wish to pay to him a tribute of sympathy. But we are also in a mood of determination and resolution.

"The Deputy-Leader of the Opposition referred to the atmosphere of anger and apprehension which reigned in the House on Saturday.

"To-day the atmosphere is happily changed, yet underneath those two phases of mood is the reality of our determination to see this thing through.

"The Deputy-Leader of the Opposition has paid eloquent tribute to the restraint with which Poland has behaved during these last few weeks and the bravery which her troops are now showing.

"Let me associate myself in full with the eloquent tribute on behalf of my friends and myself which the Deputy-Leader of the Opposition paid to the Polish people and the Polish Parliament.

"Let me pay my tribute to the people of France who have for so long been making such great preparations for the struggle with which we are now faced.

"I do not say that in organisation we yield anything to them. Great advances have been made in our organisation for war, but in the individual preparation in the contribution which the men and women of the two countries are now making to the common cause I say that France at this moment are ahead of us."

"If you go to France and meet ten people in the street you may be sure that eight of them have their place or their parts to play. Our people will do the same when the time comes, but let us have no doubt about the determination with which the French people are facing this crisis. (Cheers.)

"Let me say in conclusion that the world knows that the British people are inexorably determined, as the Prime Minister said, to end this Nazi domination forever and to build an order based on justice and freedom in Europe." (Cheers.)

MR. CHURCHILL'S SPEECH.

Mr. WINSTON CHURCHILL (C., Epping Forest) said:

"In this solemn hour it is a consolation to recall and to dwell upon our repeated efforts for peace.

"All have been ill-starred but all have been faithful and sincere. This is of the highest moral value (hear hear) and not only moral value but of practical value at the present time because of the whole-hearted concurrence of scores of millions of men and women whose co-operation is indispensable, whose comradeship and brotherhood is indispensable.

"That is the only foundation upon which the trials and tribulations of modern war can be endured and surmounted.

"This moral conviction alone affords that ever fresh resilience which renews the strength and energy of peoples in long and doubtful and dark days.

"Outside the storms of war might blow and the land may be lashed with the fury of its gale but in our own hearts this Sunday morning there is peace. (Cheers).

"Our hands may be active but our consciences are at rest. (Cheers).

"Let us not mistake the gravity of the task which lies before us, the severity of the ordeal to which we shall not be found unequal.

"We must expect many disappointments and many unpleasant surprises, but we may be sure that the task which we have really accepted is one not beyond the compass of the strength of the British Empire and the French Republic.

"The Prime Minister said it was a sad day, and that indeed is true, but it seems to me there is another note which may be present at this moment.

"That is a feeling of thankfulness that if these trials were to come upon our island there is a generation of Britons here now ready to prove it is not unworthy of the days of yore, not unworthy of those great men, the fathers of our land."

FIGHTING TO SAVE THE WORLD.

There is no question of fighting for Danzig or fighting for Poland. We are fighting to save the world from the pestilence of Nazi tyranny —(cheers)—and defence of all that is most sacred to man.

This is no war for domination, for Imperial aggrandisement, for material gain, no war to shut any country out of its sunlight and means of progress. It is a war pure in its inherent quality, a war to establish on unimpeachable rocks the rights of the individual, and it is a war to establish and revive the stature of man.

"Perhaps it may seem a paradox that a war undertaken in the name of liberty and right should require as a necessary part of its progress the surrender for the time being of so many dearly-valued liberties and rights. In these last two days the House of Commons has been voting dozens of Bills which hand over to the Executive our most dearly-valued personal liberties.

"We are sure that these liberties will be in the hands which will not abuse them; which will use them for no class or party interests—(Cheers)—which will cherish and guard them, and we look forward to the day, surely and confidently we look forward to the day, when our liberties and rights will be restored to us, and when we shall be able to share them with peoples to whom such blessings are unknown." (Loud cheers.)

THE VOICE OF CLYDESIDE.

Mr. M'GOVERN (I.L.P. Shettleston) said that this day was a most distressing and depressing one.

The I.L.P. had travelled the road of peace with the Prime Minister maligned and attacked from many quarters, but in the paths of war they regretted that they could not accompany him. The surest thing which had driven mankind along the path of war was, in his opinion, the defection of Russia.

When he heard of the Russian mobilisation on the rear of the Polish Army he could see only that, either they intended, in conjunction with Hitler, to blackmail the Poles into surrender and submission, or they intended to maintain neutrality and hold part of the Polish Army in order to aid Hitler, or they intended eventually to assist in the tearing apart of Poland along with Germany for their own aims and own use.

Mr. M'Govern added:

"If there have been any doubts in the mind of Hitler over going to war, the Soviet Government have the criminal responsibility of dissipating those doubts."

He intended to maintain his point of view.

He sympathised this morning with the millions of workers in every country that was going to be involved—the mothers, fathers, and sons in Germany, France, Austria, Poland, Great Britain and our possessions overseas.

His heart went out to every human being who was going to be affected by this tragedy, the magnitude of which no man could forsee and the end of which no man could foretell.

GENERAL CRIES OF "NO."

In these circumstances he regretted that he could not go along the road of public opinion.

"In the tragedies that follow in six months, that opinion will not be so determined, or so strong," he said. (General cries of "no.")

He hoped every person of military age who believed in giving his services would give them. (Cheers.) He regretted that after two thousand years of the Gospel of the Prince of Peace mankind on a Sunday morning should find themselves in this position.

"I cannot support this country in this catastrophe," he concluded. "I do not regard it as being idealistic; I do not regard it as being for Freedom, Justice, and Human Right. I regard it on both sides a soulless, grinding materialistic struggle for human gain and for the protection of selfish interests. In that we shall have no part, but we hope that the peoples of the world at the earliest possible moment in Germany and other countries will rise in revolt and overthrow the tyrannies that exist and will establish a real peace and comfort on earth."

MR. GEORGE LANSBURY.

Mr. GEORGE LANSBURY (Lab., Bow and Bromley) said that he hoped very much that those in charge of Government propaganda would do their best to keep down the hatred fires that were bound to arise. He also wanted to ask that the Prime Minister and the Government should again consider the question of aerial warfare, and whether even now it would not be possible to make a proposal to Germany and the world that we would be perfectly willing to abolish now aerial warfare in its entirety.

"I have just come in from an air raid shelter after the warning," he added. "What struck me was the calmness and the feeling that the Government and the country were in the right.

"I know there was also underlying it the feeling that it is a terrible thing that either young people or old people should have lived to see the day when these foul weapons are being used."

He hoped that out of this there would arise a real spirit, a spirit that would compel people to give up reliance on force.

Perhaps this time humanity would learn a lesson and refuse in the future to put its trust in poison gas in the massacre of little children and in universal hatred.

If mankind was to live in freedom and peace there was only one way in which it could do so, and that was by a complete change of mind and outlook to enable us to see ourselves in other people and God in everybody.

FORMER PRIME MINISTER.

Mr. LLOYD GEORGE (Lib., Carnarvon Burghs) said:

"I am one of those who, from time to time, have challenged the handling of foreign affairs by the Government, but this is a different matter.

"The Government are now confronted with the latest, but I am afraid not the last, of a series of acts of brigandage by a very formidable military Power which, if they are left unchallenged, will undermine the whole foundations of civilisation.

(Continued on Page 2, Column 5.)

In the City Hall. The Banqueting Chamber, scene of many historic functions, bore the brunt of the damage.

The remarkable photographs on this and the following page were taken by a " Telegraph " photographer during the height of the raid.

Top—Billowing flames at the corner of Rosemary Street and North Street.

Bottom—Caught in the maelstrom. Looking from North Street towards the " Northern Whig " Office in Bridge Street.

Crumlin Road Presbyterian Church outlined in fire.

A stretcher party passing the church on their errand of mercy.

In Castle Street, where several blocks were gutted.

Top—Section of the roof of the Belfast City Hall above the Banqueting Chamber.
Bottom—Queen's University students helping to clear up Eglinton Street.

Firemen quelling an outbreak in High Street.

Hoses playing on a collapsed building in Victoria Street (Ann Street corner).

High Street. The arrows in upper picture indicate the area on which bombs fell, and in the lower the corresponding space after raids.

As it was after being blitzed.

The cleared area is given over to air raid shelters, military car park, a gospel tent and static water tank.

More views of High Street——before and after.

From base of Albert Memorial.

Cleared area, corner of High Street and Victoria Street.

The narrowness of the escape of St. Anne's Cathedral, Donegall Street, can be judged from this picture.

The International Bar (corner of Donegall Street and York Street) still ablaze.

The same site after clearance showing a new side view of the Cathedral from the corner of Royal Avenue.

The Royal Avenue end of York Street as it appeared after the raid.

The facade of the '' International '' before being pulled down.

The same area cleared. Note the single shop, still open for business.

The section of High Street from National Bank to Curley's Buildings.

Albert Square and Tomb Street. Messrs. J. & T. Sinclair's extensive curing premises seen down the street, were also gutted.

Corner of High Street and Victoria Street.

New vistas. Citizens can now see the time by the " Albert " from Waring Street.

Arthur Street, as seen from Donegall Place. The gap has been created by the destruction of Messrs. Brand's (Ulster Arcade) Emporium.

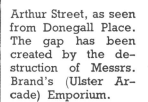

High Street.

The remains of an air raid shelter in Thorndyke Street. In the background streets of houses wrecked by blast.

Smoke still rises from a bomb crater in Halliday's Road.

A.R.P. An auxiliary water main in Chichester Street.

The " Belfast Telegraph " Office, Royal Avenue. Every window, both inside and out, was shattered by blast from bombs which narrowly missed the building.

" Boarded up "—but still going strong. The three Belfast morning papers were also published here for a period following the raid.

New vistas ! Donegall Place as seen from Arthur Street.

The corner of Victoria Street and Waring Street as seen from the '' Albert.''

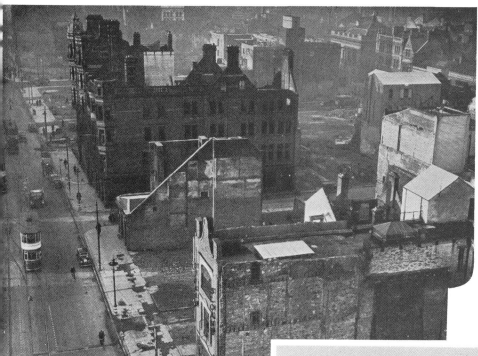

This view of High Street from the Albert Memorial presents an impressive picture of destruction in the heart of the City.

Bridge Street, one of the City's oldest and busiest thoroughfares, still does duty as a connecting link.

Another view of Bridge Street, looking from North Street into High Street.

Another part of old Belfast which came to grief. The wreckage of Rosemary Street, as glimpsed from Waring Street.

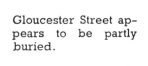

Gloucester Street appears to be partly buried.

Sugarhouse Entry, where the United Irishmen used to meet under the leadership of Henry Joy McCracken in the days of '98.

"Mopping up" operations in High Street.

typical aftermath— corner of High eet and Bridge St.

A steamroller is pressed into service for pulling down buildings in Waring Street.

Silhouette ! A water tower in Castle Lane with flame-lit sky for background.

One of Belfast' new "wide ope spaces " — cleare area, Bridge Stree

Demolition work in Bridge Street.

An old-established firm "crashes."
Bringing down Haslett's premises in
North Street.

Another view of de-
bris-strewn Bridge St.
from the Belfast Bank.

The largest of its kind in the world, York Street
Flax Spinning Co., Ltd.'s plant before the blitz.

The site as it is to-day. The great mill chimney is all that is left of the massive
undertaking. Gallaher's famous tobacco factory is seen in new perspective.

The rear of "York Street Mill" in North Queen Street, where Grove Street and Vere St. intersect. Mounds of rubble mark where rows of workers' dwellings once stood.

The view from Henry Street with smoke and flame still rising from portions of the mill premises.

Part of the mill frontage on York Street, each floor bearing its complement of machinery now reduced to scrap.

A. "bird's-eye" view of the L M S N C C passenger platforms, York Rd. terminus.

The Goods Yard littered with twisted steelwork.

The station frontage on York Road.

L.M.S. station. Wrecked goods trains in a marshalling yard.

L M S Hotel. One of the City's leading hotels; it was completely destroyed.

A departure platform minus its glass roof.

L M S station. Another
section of the exterior which
received damage.

A breakdown gang dis-
posing of debris in the
goods yard.

Another part of the yard
being cleared for traffic.

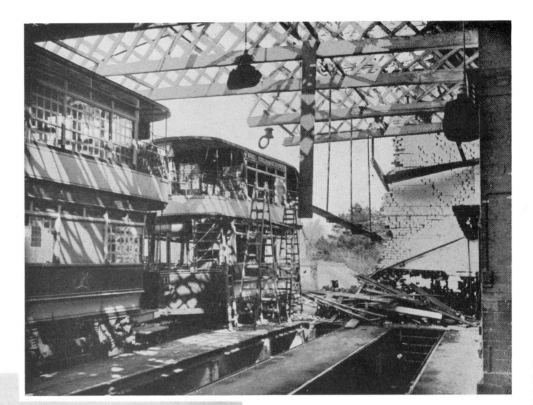

The Municipal tram service carried on despite handicaps imposed by Hitler's bombs, which fell both inside and outside this depot in Salisbury Avenue (Antrim Road).

The stuff to give 'em ! Ballymoney
mobile canteen treats the troops to
a welcome cup of tea.

Children being evacuated after the
April blitz.

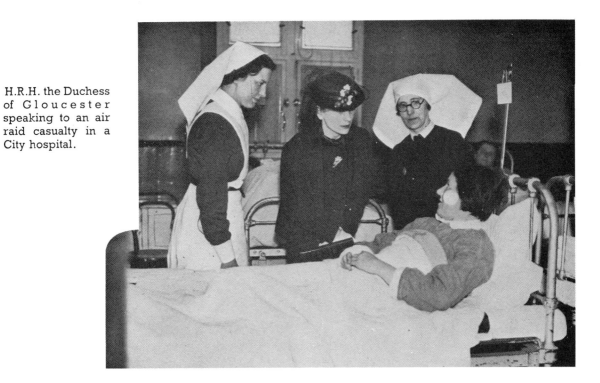

H.R.H. the Duchess of Gloucester speaking to an air raid casualty in a City hospital.

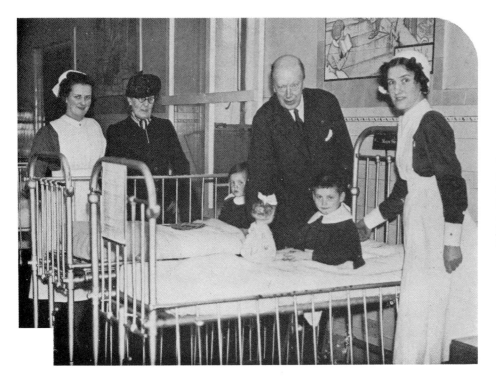

Their Graces the Governor of Northern Ireland and the Duchess of Abercorn visit injured in the Children's Hospital.

Musical interlude.
An impromptu organ recital in York Road.

Blitzed dwellings in Whitewell Road.

Left—The damaged interior of St. Patrick's Parish Church, Ballymacarrett.

Below—Oldpark Presbyterian Church, Cliftonville Road.

Spamount Congregational Church, North Queen Street.

Bomb crater at St. Matthew's R.C. Church, Newtownards Road.

St. Barnabas Parish Church,
Duncairn Gardens.

Duncairn Gardens Methodist
Church.

Newtownards Road
Methodist Church.

York Street Presbyterian Church.

York Street Non-Subscribing Presbyterian Church.

Castleton Presbyterian Church, York Road.

St. Silas's Parish Church, Oldpark Road.

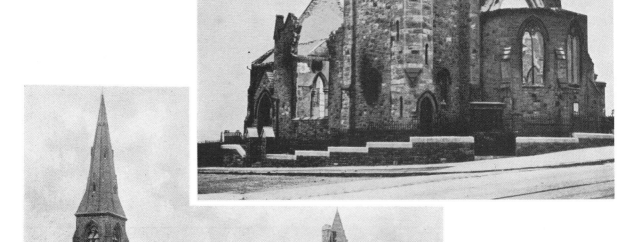

St. James's Parish Church and Schools, Antrim Road.

Chancel of St. James's before the blitz.

The facade and interior of Rosemary Street Presbyterian Church following the blitz, with a view of the interior as it was

—and after.

Clifton Street Presbyterian Church
before——

Holy Trinity Parish Church, off Clifton
Street, minus its familiar spire.

Newington Presbyterian Church,
Limestone Road.

Two more "before and after" studies. Macrory Memorial Presbyterian Church, Duncairn Gardens.

Donegall Street Congregational Church which had only been erected in 1934 on the site of the original edifice, also destroyed by fire.

Top—Tower Street has disappeared, but St. Patrick's Church tower, from which it got its name, still stands foursquare. Westbourne Street was also destroyed, and the ruins of Templemore Avenue Library are seen at right centre.

Bottom—Tamar Street and Dee Street, Newtownards Road, experienced the full force of the blitz. The area is here shown partly cleared, with air raid shelters taking the place of demolished houses.

Only the walls remain of Strand Public Elementary School.

Section of a gigantic bomb crater in Ravenscroft Avenue, Newtownards Road, where there were numerous casualties.

Clearance work in progress at East Bridge Street.

A bomb crater on Cliftonville Road. Blast destroyed a number of premises in the vicinity.

All that was left of modern villa residences in Sunningdale Park, Cavehill Road.

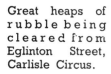

Great heaps of rubble being cleared from Eglinton Street, Carlisle Circus.

Top—Another view of the damage in Eglinton Street.

Centre—Another view of Sunningdale Park.

Heavy bombs fell at the junction of Antrim Road and Duncairn Gardens, demolishing a number of houses.

Top—Whitewell Road. Many dwellings here were razed to the ground.

Centre— A.F.S. who rendered invaluable aid in fighting outbreaks of fire and in rescue work, being inspected by Rt. Hon. J. C. MacDermott, K.C. (then Minister of Public Security)

A vacant space in York Road with Castleton Presbyterian Church in background.

Wrecked houses and a wrecked car in Hughenden Avenue, Cavehill Road.

Blitz – scarred Shandarragh Park, Cavehill Road.

Destruction in Atlantic Avenue, Antrim Road, with all that remained of an air raid shelter.

Top—Amateurs! Students from Queen's University, Belfast, assisting in pulling down houses in Eglinton Street.

Bottom—Professionals! Sappers clearing debris in Walton Street, Crumlin Road.

Top—Salvaging furniture at Southport Street and Manor Street corner (Oldpark Road).

Bottom—Auxiliary firemen fighting the flames in York Street.

Eglinton Street and Carlisle Street (Carlisle Circus) after being cleared.

Where a heavy bomb fell. Wrecked houses on the Antrim Road between Duncairn Gardens and Hillman Street.

The Union Jac expresses th "morning after spirit in Annadal Street (Antrin Road).

Partially cleared area, Ballycarry and Ballynure Streets.

Annadale St., Antrim Road, where every house was destroyed.

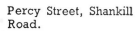

Percy Street, Shankill Road.

Top—York Street and Great Patrick Street.

Bottom—Soldiers, here seen hard at work in York Street, rendered yeoman service throughout the city.

A block of shops at Newcastle Street on Newtownards Road which came to grief.

The Duke and Duchess of Gloucester inspecting the damage in Percy Street.

Ravenscroft Avenue, Bloomfield, where a number of the residents were killed.

City Hospitals suffered grievously in the blitz, among them the Ulster Hospital for Women and Children, Templemore Avenue.

Front and rear views of the Hospital, showing the Hun's handiwork.

The Police Court, Chichester Street, in front of which a bomb exploded.

Templemore Avenue branch cf Belfast Public Library.

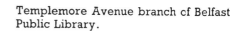

Household effects being salved from dwellings in Westbourne Street, Newtownards Road. Note the Union Jack.

Pathetic pilgrimage! Homeless people return to search the ruins of their dwellings in Annadale St., Antrim Road.

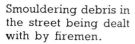
Smouldering debris in the street being dealt with by firemen.

Levelled off! The street as it appears now.

"Big open spaces!" Corner of Victoria Street and Ann Street.

Between Duncairn Gardens and Hillman Street (Antrim Road).

Newtownards Road, where the Methodist Church once stood.

Pack up your——personal effects ! Householders of Ballyclare Street, Oldpark Road, " evacuating " their possessions.

A booklover in Roseleigh Street, (Oldpark Road—Cliftonville).

On the way to safety. A trio—or should it be a quartette !

The Corporals' mess ! Military Police pause for a snack.

In the heart of Belfast, where well–remembered landmarks stood, the last
'' All Clear '' will be the signal for the citizens to begin the work of building
anew.

There is a surprising dearth of information available on the blitz. This is the only book which deals specifically with the events of April/May 1941. There are, nevertheless, a number of minor sources. Most biographies of Northern Ireland personalities make reference to the bombings. In addition, diaries and letters are an invaluable source.

Official documents and papers give an indication of the government response both to the prospect of war and the aftermath of each Luftwaffe raid. Cabinet papers, official reports, minutes of meetings and United Kingdom Regulations are all readily available – primarily in the Public Record Office of Northern Ireland. In addition, the Belfast blitz was raised in parliament both at Stormont and Westminster and in Dail Eireann.

The historians' usual source for Twentieth Century history – contemporary newspaper sources – are virtually valueless. This was due to official censorship. It was felt that to dwell on civilian casualties would be detrimental to morale and to list industrial targets destroyed would offer the Germans valuable information. *Bombs on Belfast*, for example, when it first appeared was permitted only a paragraph foreward. In addition not one photograph of industrial damage can be found throughout the book.

Fortunately each of the Belfast newspapers, *Northern Whig*, *Belfast News Letter*, *Irish News* and *Belfast Telegraph* produced supplements for the twentieth anniversary of the blitz in May 1961. These, at least, were free from the pressure of the censor.

The most valuable source for further research, used extensively for this work, will almost certainly prove to be oral history accounts. Much of the minutiae of the blitz is available only through the medium of the spoken word. The real history of the blitz is the story of the suffering of the citizens of Belfast; it is they who can fully explain the events of May 1941. In a city better known for its self-inflicted wounds the German Luftwaffe dealt a common blow to the two communities. In this, at least, we had something in common.

Christopher D. McGimpsey
Ballyhackamore Village
Belfast
18 October 1988

Select Bibliography

BARDON, Jonathan, *Belfast; An Illustrated History* (Belfast, 1982).
BARTON, Brian, 'The Belfast Blitz', in, *North Belfast Historical Magazine* (No. 1, 1984) pp 34–38.
BLAKE, J. W., *Northern Ireland in the Second World War* HMSO (London, 1956).
DAVISON, Robson, *The German Air-raids on Belfast of April and May, 1941, and their consequences*, unpublished PhD Thesis (QUB, 1979).
FISK, Robert, *In Time of War; Ireland, Ulster and the Price of Neutrality, 1939–45* (London, 1983).
MOORE, Brian, *The Emperor of Ice-cream* (London, 1966).
ULSTER YEAR BOOK, 1947, HMSO (Belfast, 1947).